freebie.robloxiakid.com/r

**UNOFFICIAL**

**GRANNY**

**BOOK 1**
**ROBLOXIA KID**

# Contents

My dearest fans
and reviewers:

ROBLOXIA KID

Y T A H A
Coolalto940
Diamondminer168
Dragonfire
Tobi Salami
Ellen Henry
Natalija F.
JV

THANK YOU!!!

Prologue

# A Bear Trap in More Ways Than One.

When faced with your imminent end, a lot of things can run through your mind. Good thoughts, bad thoughts, crazy thoughts... a lot of random thoughts can pop up. I guess that's just the way it is. I mean, when you're at the edge and about to die, what else can you do?

So, there I was, the strong bear trap clamped firmly onto my leg. Its large metal claws had popped up out of nowhere. Let me tell you now, it felt beyond painful; I can't describe just how agonizing it was. The metal clamps bit into these short and blocky legs of mine, and I was going nowhere.

"Argh! I can't move! Help! Help!"

I called out for help, but none of my friends answered. I tried to move my leg, but the bear trap just bit more firmly into it. The room was so dark that I had walked right into Granny's infamous bear trap without realizing. I had heard stories of how players sucked into Granny's home ran into one of these things and got stuck, eventually meeting their end. Despite such tales, I never could have imagined just how dreadful this actually was. I was now experiencing the trap first-hand, and believe me, it was not fun.

There was no way I was moving from that spot. Just when I thought things couldn't get any worse I suddenly heard a low growl from a short distance in front of me. The growl didn't sound welcoming at all.

The room I had entered had been dimly-lit, its darkness concealing the bear trap. Now, I was starting to realize that there was more than just the bear trap to worry about. I looked straight ahead, and saw two red eyes staring back at me from the darkness.

"Uh oh."

Slowly, the animal emerged from the darkness. I could see it a lot clearer now, and I realized what it was. It was a large bear. The bear was huge in stature, but it was actually pretty thin. I could see its ribs sticking out from its fur. Its mouth was frothing, dripping with saliva, and it was staring right at me. This animal had not eaten for a long time, and I was its next meal.

The bear was looking right at me now and I could hear its stomach growl with anticipation. My leg was still held painfully in place by the bear trap. Yup, this was not good. In fact, it was probably one of the scariest situations I had ever found myself in.

"Nice bear. Nice bear. You wouldn't want to eat me. There are a lot of high-level Roblox players out there. They're fatter, have a lot more meat, and would taste a lot better too. And..."

The bear cut me short as it snarled and growled at me. It flashed its claws towards me, and I could see just how sharp they were. Images of being cut up and chewed up by that thing ran quickly through my head, and I screamed out desperately for help.

"No, no! Help! Decks! Dan! Tina! Anyone! Help me!"

That was when the bear rushed towards me, its claws and teeth exposed. I heard its deafening growl and I closed my eyes. I knew that I was done for now.

Suddenly, everything seemed to be happening in slow motion. The bear was still rushing right at me, but it seemed to be slowing to a crawl. My thoughts all played out in front of me, and the one thing that I kept repeating in my head was,

"How did I get into this mess?"

Entry #1

# The Mysterious House

Okay, where do I start? Well, first of all, this was definitely one of the wackiest and most off-the-wall games I had ever played in Roblox. And that's saying a lot. I've played more than my fair share of games and I've seen all kinds of stuff, from the weird to the wild to everything in between. That being said, I'd never played anything like Granny, which was, without a doubt, the creepiest and nuttiest game in Roblox. Oh, and did I mention the scariest? Well, what can I say? I didn't even want to play it. The game just sucked me and a bunch of other players into it, and that's where our story and my scariest ever diary begins. Welcome to Noob's diary in Granny!

So how did I end up playing Granny? Well, that's the thing: I didn't really want to play Granny at all. I had heard scary stories about this game in Roblox, a server that was unlike any other. While other servers were cities or even worlds that were larger than life, I'd heard that Granny was nothing more than a house. Yeah, it was a big house all right, but I'd heard that the size only made it scarier. That's because the house was so big that players regularly got lost and never returned once they were inside the huge, creepy place. I'd also heard about players getting sucked into the house for no reason. Apparently, the house was drawing players into itself like some kind of vacuum cleaner or black hole. No one really knew what type of force was at fault, but it was there, and it was doing its dirty work.

Like all bad news you hear, I didn't really pay much attention to any of it. I certainly never thought it would happen to me. No way! I just kept on living my life and chilling, not knowing that Granny would eventually suck me in, and I would find myself right in the middle of all of it. Then again, isn't that always the story of my little Roblox life?

I was in the middle of playing Mad City when it happened. Yeah, Mad City was another pretty crazy server at Roblox. I had heard about how there were a lot of gangs in Mad City that were always at odds with the cops. Shootouts, robberies, all of that was pretty common stuff for Mad City. So why would I even think of playing in that server, you ask? Well, that's just me. That's the Noobster for you. I live for action and adventure! Aaaand,

I often get what I want. In spades.

"All right, rookie. So, it's your first day at Mad City! What do you expect?"

I enlisted at the Mad City police department to get some action going. Yeah, I know it was a pretty crazy idea trying to be a cop, especially in Mad City of all places! My partner, Kenny, liked to chat a lot, and he always had two things with him: his pistol and a doughnut It was my first routine patrol and Kenny was driving the squad car while I sat beside him. I had no idea how the car could support both of us: Kenny was a heavyweight of sorts, and it showed with his round belly.

"It's Noob, not rookie."

Kenny laughed.

"Same thing to me. Want some doughnut?"

Kenny offered me a bite of his half-bitten doughnut. I could see the grease, chocolate and custard filling dripping down the sides. Kenny was getting a lot of grease on his hand as he held that half-eaten thing. It was anything but appetizing. Of course, I declined.

"Uh, no thanks! I'll pass on that."

Kenny shrugged his shoulders.

"Hey, food is food. You're going to need a lot of food to get through Mad City, believe me."

That was when we heard a shot ring out.

"There you go! Just what I was talking about. There's never a dull moment in this town, kid!"

"That sounded pretty close by."

"I think it came from the hardware store at the corner of the block."

Kenny had an unusual radar-type sense for

these things. We turned the corner and saw two perps holding up the hardware store, just like Kenny had said.

"Whoa! How did you know it was here?"

"You get used to these things when you've worked here as long as I have. And a doughnut helps. A lot."

I would have to take Kenny's advice a little more seriously. We stepped out of the car and packed our guns; it was time to get to work.

"Mad City police! Drop your weapons! Come out the store with your hands up!"

I shouted at the perps with as much authority and intimidation as I could muster. I sounded confident, but I was shaking in my boots.

"We ain't coming outside for no coppers! Screw you!"

Well, so much for negotiations. The perps were crouching behind the front desk of the hardware store. I wasn't sure if the owner had been shot or not.

Kenny and I stood outside the store. Using the corner wall for cover, we waited, ready for anything.

"This looks bad. Stay sharp," Kenny ordered.

The perps started firing first. Safe behind our cover, the bullets flew right past us, but we couldn't stay there forever. We had to make a move.

I stepped out from behind the wall and fired a few shots back. Their bullets came a lot closer to me than I wanted them to.

"Are you trying to get yourself killed? Those perps are playing for keeps! Stay covered. Those perps look real serious. I'll dash back to the car and radio for some backup. I think we'll need it."

I heard Kenny, but I couldn't just stand there and do nothing while they pinned us down. Well, actually I probably could have but I was just too cocky. A veteran cop in one of the most notorious cities in Roblox, Kenny gave great advice. Advice that I definitely should have listened to, but I didn't.

I stepped out from my cover, and tried to fire again. I figured I could take on these perps, and get some kind of citation. Just imagine! A new cop at Mad City stopping a robbery. I would be a hero! I would be famous! Yeah, keep dreaming, Noob. This time, I paid for my brashness. I felt the shot hit me, knocking me backwards.

I lost consciousness and everything went black. The last thing I heard was Kenny. I heard him talking to me, but it was too late.

"What did you do, Noob? I told you to stay in

cover!"

Yeah, those were the last things I heard before the darkness closed in on me, like a pair of dark hands covering my eyes. I didn't expect to wake up after that. I figured I was done for, and I had no one to blame but myself.

I woke up with a major headache. My head felt like someone had played several games of soccer with it and I could barely get up. Somehow, I managed to open my eyes and take a look around me.

"Ouch! My head! What happened? Wait, I remember! I just got shot! I'm supposed to be outside the hardware store. Where am I?"

I looked around at my surroundings. I definitely wasn't outside the hardware store anymore. Instead, I was inside what appeared to be an old, rotting house. The paint on the walls was peeling off, and the floorboards looked so unstable and creaky that I was reluctant to stand on them. There were cobwebs everywhere and I thought I would choke with all the dust in the air. On the opposite wall, a pair of shattered windows were boarded up, and the bulb above us flickered on and off, barely giving out any light. What kind of place was this?

There were several other players in the room too. Like me, they were all just waking up. One of them was even pretty famous. I had seen him play in several servers and he often liked to post vids about his game experiences.

"Danny SN? Is that you? What are you doing here?"

"Hey, aren't you Noob?"

It was Danny. He actually recognized me! Despite meeting in such a scary situation, I found that very cool. I was really surprised that a famous Roblox-er like Danny SN knew me. For a moment, all my confusion and tension vanished.

"Whoa! You recognize me? I mean, you're Danny SN!"

"And you're Noob! I mean, I played a few servers you were in. I actually bumped into you before and I've got to say I liked what I saw back then."

I was happy to see that Danny was a cool and nice guy. It was wonderful that he knew and remembered me.

"Gee, thanks, Danny! I'm surprised you even remember me."

"I try to make a point of remembering every player I play with. After all, we're all really just trying to have fun, right?"

"Sorry to disappoint you, guys, but I don't think we're going to have fun here. I'm pretty sure this is Granny's house!

One of the other players in the house spoke up. She sounded really scared, and I couldn't blame her. After all, this was Granny; none of us wanted to be here or to face her.

"Casey's right! We were sucked into this place by Granny! Man, I've heard about players getting sucked into this game and never coming back. I heard she just sucks players from their servers at random, and brings them over to her place here. I never thought that I would actually become one of those victims. I'm Decks, by the way."

"Nice to meet you guys. I'm Noob. I'm a cop at Mad City. I was actually trying to stop a hardware store robbery when I got shot and ended up here. Hang on a minute! I was shot! I was shot! Why am I not shot anymore?"

"I hear Granny has all sorts of crazy powers. Your wound must have healed when you got sucked in here. Unfortunately, Granny's crazy, and she's going to do a lot more than just shoot you."

That was when we saw a huge figure dart out from the corner of the room. The figure was dark and I couldn't make out who, or what, it was. I instinctively reached for my gun on my hip. My hand fumbled around but found nothing.

"What is that thing?"

"I don't know! But someone's got to do something! You're a cop, Noob! Shoot it!" Danny ordered.

"I would if I had my gun! It's gone!"

We all thought that it was Granny, and that she was going to cut us up, or worse. Nothing of the sort happened.

"Will you guys get a grip? It's nothing! Just a spider," Decks said.

Decks was right. It was just a spider darting from one cobweb to another. The dim and flickering light cast it with a huge shadow, making it look massive for a moment.

Decks sounded really calm and level-headed. With an attitude like that, he would have made a better cop than I did in Mad City.

"No need to scare the cop, Casey. We were all minding our own business until Granny came and dragged us here. We have to find a way out!" Decks said.

"That's going to be a lot easier said than done, Decks. I've heard that this house may seem small on the outside, but it's a lot larger than it looks on the inside. A lot of players have found themselves lost in Granny's place, never to return again."

"Don't remind us all, Dan. We all know that this is a pretty bad situation. We just have to stay positive and try to find a way to get out of here," Casey replied.

Casey was right. It was bad. What we didn't know at that point though was that it was about to get a whole lot worse.

"Well, we all agree that we have to get out of this house. The question is, how are we going to do that when we can't get out of this room?"

Dan was right. We were locked in. Just as we were discussing the problem, however, we heard a clicking sound and the door slowly opened. We looked at each other with confusion and suspicion.

"That door was locked! Why is it suddenly open now?" Decks exclaimed.

"Something's definitely not right about the door opening just like that. It's almost as if Granny wants to get us out of this room."

"She wants to hunt us down like some kind

of sport," Casey agreed.

Dan shrugged his shoulders.

"Probably so, but we really don't have much of a choice. We can't stay in this room forever."

Dan had a point. If we went outside, we were definitely taking a big risk of running into Granny, who was almost certainly lurking in the house somewhere. However, staying in the room was not an option either.

"I guess we really don't have a choice. We have to try to get out of here," Casey reasoned.

"Yeah. I better go out first. I'm the biggest dude around here."

Decks was right. He was pretty big, but I also could tell that he was scared out of his mind at being the first to step outside. Since he was so big though, he was probably the one who could best handle himself should things get out of hand.

"We're right behind you, Decks," Dan said.

The four of us slowly moved towards the door. Just as he had promised, Decks was the first in line. He slowly pulled on the handle of the door and opened it fully. The door squeaked and creaked and really needed some oiling.

"The coast is clear, guys. There's no sign of creepy Granny anywhere," Decks confirmed.

"Well, let's get moving then while we can," Dan responded.

We were surprised to walk out of the room without anything happening. We had expected Granny to come out of nowhere, but she didn't. I guess she was biding time before she made her first move.

The room opened onto a long hallway with

several other doors. Suddenly, we heard several voices coming from another room.

"Is somebody out there? Help!"

The voices came from behind one of the closed doors.

"There are other players here too!" I said.

"We better open that door."

I pulled on the door but it was locked. I realized that we were not going to be able to open this door in the normal way.

"Please, you have to help me! I don't want to be locked in this room forever!"

"Take it easy! We're going to get you out of there," I shouted back.

"The door's locked. I'm going to have to kick it down."

None of us doubted that Decks could do just that. After all, he was pretty big and strong-looking. He raised his foot and pulled it back. Taking a deep breath, he kicked down the door with one powerful push, sending it flying.

"It's open! Come on!"

Decks rushed into the room, and we followed. There were other Roblox players inside. They all looked pretty relieved to see us and seemed just as frightened as we were.

"Thank goodness! I knew there were other people aside from us in here!"

"How long have you guys been here?" Decks asked.

"I don't know. If you guys are like us, then you would have just been minding your own business, then suddenly you woke up here in this place. We were all locked up in this room together. I'm assuming you guys had a similar experience? I'm Shelby, by the way, and these are my friends: Carlos, Pitt, Dickie and Tina.

Shelby looked like a real smart guy, while his friends all looked like your average Roblox player. They were all pretty afraid and in shock at what had happened. Yeah, they were much like us. They were all just chilling and playing, doing their own thing, until the mysterious force that was Granny whisked them away and brought them here. Yeah, we were all pretty unlucky all right.

"Well, I'm Decks, this is Danny SN, that's Casey and this is Noob. It looks like we were all brought together by Granny somehow."

"I've heard a lot of bad stuff about Granny," Carlos admitted.

"We all have. We've all heard about the mysterious force taking Roblox players and sending them to this old and dingy house. I never expected to end up a victim myself though."

"None of us did. We'll all just have to work together to get out of here," I replied.

"Exactly. We better stay together and keep moving. Maybe we'll find a way out of this place."

"Sorry, but that doesn't sound like much of a plan," Pitt said snidely.

Dan looked at him with annoyance for a moment before answering.

"All right. Maybe it isn't much, but do you have any better ideas?"

Pitt didn't answer, and neither did his friends. I guess that was their answer. They really didn't have much of a choice; we would all have to stick together if we wanted to have a chance of getting out of this crazy place in one piece.

"Come on. We better get moving," Decks insisted.

So, there we were. Several players all stumbling around in one group, trying to find a way out of the crazy, maze-like house. It wouldn't be easy to find the exit, especially knowing that Granny was sure to strike at any moment.

Entry #2

# Exploring Granny's Creepy House.

We wandered around the house for what seemed like forever. Each door seemed to look just like the one before it. The whole wall was like a giant snake that slithered around in a long and endless loop.

"Where are we going? Each door seems to be the same, and the walls seem to go around in circles. This whole dingy house feels like a cramped maze!" Shelby exclaimed.

"I know! We've been at this forever! And

Granny hasn't even made her move yet," Tina whined.

"This is getting crazy. We have to do something other than wander around the house like this," Dan agreed.

He was right. If we kept at this, we would never find the way out. We were like little mice going around in circles, and I couldn't shake the feeling that this was exactly how Granny wanted it to be.

"How about we open each door we see?" I volunteered.

"Good thinking, Noob! Let's do that! It's better than wandering around in circles like this," Dan replied.

It was the only logical solution. After all, we couldn't keep going around like this. We had to do something to help us find the way out.

"No way! We don't even know what's behind

those doors. One of those rooms is bound to contain a trap... maybe more than one. Who knows what's lurking behind those doors?" Casey argued.

"No, I agree with Dan and Noob. We're never going to find the way out or discover anything useful if we don't open more doors," Decks said.

No one really liked the idea of opening doors or breaking down locked ones to see what was behind them. The whole house was just plain creepy. Still, no one said anything after Decks spoke. Everyone knew that we didn't really have any choice. It was either explore and risk getting hurt, or just wander around in circles indefinitely.

"You guys are right. We should start opening doors, even if it's scary," Dicky agreed.

"It seems like we're all kind of in agreement then," Tina said.

"Alright, so we open doors. Who's going to stay in front and take the biggest risk?"

"I will. I am the biggest anyway, and I already kicked your door down," Decks said.

No one tried to say otherwise. I was glad that Decks was willing to take the risk. If he wasn't, I really wasn't sure who would go up front.

"Well, we might as well start with this door here," Pitt said, pointing at the door right in front of us. It was closed, like all the other doors in that creepy place. Decks stepped forward with no sign of fear or hesitation.

"All right, I'm opening it. You guys had better step back or something."

"I'll come with you. It's better that you go in with some help," Shelby offered.

Decks nodded and gripped the doorknob.

"On three. One, two..."

Decks turned the doorknob. It wasn't locked. The door opened easily, and the two of them stepped into the room. The room was pitch black, and we all had no idea who, or what, was inside. It could have been Granny in that room for all we knew. I have to admit, Decks and Shelby really had a lot of guts stepping into the room like that. It was like stepping into the unknown, literally.

"All right, turn on the light!" Decks ordered.

I fumbled for the light switch just inside the door and flicked it on. A bright light came over the room. It was a kitchen. There was a stove under an old. The countertop had not been used or cleaned in a while, and it was grimy and covered in dust. There were shelves and cupboards that looked very old. It also smelled quite bad. It really should have been cleaned a long time ago, but I was sure that Granny wasn't one for cleaning around the house. By now, we were all sure that Granny was not one to care much about keeping her house in order.

"That's one awfully dirty kitchen! I sure wouldn't want to let my kitchen get like that!" Tina exclaimed.

"I have to confess that my kitchen kind of ended up this dirty once," Casey said.

"Hey, guys, you can compare home-making notes later. Maybe we should all just focus on finding something useful in here," Dan said.

He was right. It was time to get serious and start looking for items that could really be of use against Granny. After all, from the stories we'd heard about her, she was very dangerous, and we had to be ready for anything.

"I've got a rolling pin. This might come in handy," I said.

The rolling pin was large and made of wood. It was good for rolling dough, but it would also make a good weapon if needs be. Just thinking about it made me squirm a little. I didn't want to use a cooking utensil for such a purpose, but I really didn't have much of a choice. None of us did.

"This might come in handy too," Dick said.

He grabbed a frying pan. I figured he had the same idea as I did with the rolling pin.

"I guess this kettle ought to do," Casey said.

"What's that supposed to do if Granny attacks?" Dan asked.

"The kettle is full of boiling water. You wouldn't want any of this splashed on your face, right? I figure Granny won't want any of it on her face either."

"Ouch."

"This oven mitt might be... well, it might be a good boxing glove for fighting Granny," Pitt said.

"Were you ever good at any kind of fighting?" Carlos asked.

"Not really, but I'm sure this mitten will be good enough for an old woman like her. I mean, it's sure to hurt if I punch her with it!"

"Yeah, maybe so, but I wouldn't need a glove like that to get an old lady like Granny. If you ask me, I could take on anyone with my bare fists!"

Despite just meeting these people, I could tell that Carlos was the cocky type. He did not bother even trying to look for anything to help him against Granny. Instead, while we searched, he did some shadow boxing in a corner; it appeared that he really did believe that his fighting skills alone would be up to the task.

"Uhm, no offense Carlos, but are you sure that you can handle Granny? I mean, I haven't seen you fight before or anything, and I don't mean to judge, but Granny's got a pretty fearsome reputation and all," I questioned.

"Yeah, I've heard about her reputation. I've heard all sorts of crazy stories about her. I'm sure all of those stories are nothing but crazy tales to scare kids!"

"I don't know about that, Carlos. I mean..."

I was cut short as the lights suddenly went off. Casey and Tina wailed loudly and we all started shouting. It was worse than any jump scare you could imagine.

"Hey, what's going on?"

"Who turned out the lights?"

"Hey!"

I stumbled around in the dark, just like everyone else. I had no idea what was going on, and we were all pretty much terrified.

"Somebody turn on the lights!"

I heard a lot of moving and stumbling but I couldn't tell what was going on. It was like someone had tossed a giant blanket over us all, and we were just moving in the dark.

I heard Decks moving around the room. I could tell it was him because his large frame made heavy footsteps on the ground. It was like hearing a bull moving around in a china shop. I heard the flick of a switch and, finally, the lights came back on.

Everyone squinted and rubbed their eyes as light flooded the entire room again. We looked at each other; something was definitely wrong.

"Is everybody okay?" Decks asked.

"I-I think so..." Pitt said, checking himself out as if convinced there was a wound somewhere on his body.

"Oh my gosh! Where's Carlos?" Casey questioned.

Everyone stood silent and looked around. There were no signs of Carlos anywhere.

"Carlos! Where are you?" Dan shouted.

There was no reply except the echo of Dan's own voice bouncing around the entire house. There was an uneasy tension in the room. Everyone knew that something had happened to Carlos... something bad.

"Oh my gosh... Granny has made her first move... what are we going to do?! Who's going to be next? I knew this was going to end badly for me--"

"Whoa, hold up there! We're not about to leave anyone behind, you got that? We got here as a group and we're going to leave this stinking house as one!" Decks shouted, interrupting Tina's panic.

Decks was definitely the commanding presence in the group, and everyone silently acknowledged him as the leader of our little pack. We all silently nodded our heads in agreement.

"Decks is right. We just need to calm down. I'm sure Carlos is around here somewhere; we've just got to know where to look for him," I said calmly.

Shelby had seemed awfully quiet this whole time and I caught him shaking his head.

"Shelby, what's wrong?" I asked him.

"I don't know, dude. I think I've seen this before in a video... Granny strikes when everyone least expects it... Carlos is a goner, I'm sure of it. And in time... everyone else here will be too," Shelby said grimly.

Shelby was probably one of the smarter guys in the room, and those words coming from him didn't make any of us feel any better.

"Hey, if you're going to be so negative the whole time, then you can stay here in the kitchen and mope all day while you wait for that old hag to get you! Otherwise, gather up all the stuff you might need from here and follow me!" Decks commanded.

Before anyone else had time to say anything, we heard the sudden sound of heavy footsteps in the distance. All our heads turned in the direction of the sound. There was no mistaking it; it was definitely Granny. I mean, who else could it have been? Unless some random dude had decided to take a relaxing stroll around this creepy house, it could only mean one thing.... Granny was nearby.

"W-who was that?!" Tina shouted.

I could tell that she was starting to get really scared by everything that was happening. I mean, we were all scared, no doubt about it. Who wouldn't be, right? But Tina was the worst of us all. It's almost as if I could smell the fear coming from her body! I bet she didn't like watching scary movies and stuff like that.

"Granny! Who else could it be? We'd better go check it out!" Decks said.

"Wait! What if that was Carlos?" Pitt replied.

"Impossible! We called for Carlos earlier and he didn't say a thing! That can't have been him!"

"Look, guys, I don't think it matters right now who that was. We'd better get out of this kitchen. The longer we stay here, the slimmer our chances are of breaking out of this creepy place! Let's move!" Dan ordered.

We quickly moved around the kitchen, collecting together anything we might need. I even saw Pitt snatch an oven mitt from one of the drawers before leaving the place. What on earth are you supposed to do with an oven mitt in a fight exactly?! Offer your opponent a poisonous pie? Bake them to death? It was a really weird weapon of choice if you ask me; Pitt would have been better off taking a fork, or even a small glass. But that was his choice, and I guess it was still better than what Carlos did: arrogantly not picking anything at all because he thought he was tough enough to fight Granny with his bare fists.

We began to exit the kitchen slowly, each of us following the person in front like a train made up of frightened people. We scanned the corridor and turned in the direction of the sound of footsteps from earlier.

Entry #3

# The Secret Door.

We were back in the same hallway again with the doors that all looked the same. Dan and Decks seemed to know where the footsteps had come from though, so they took the lead and the rest of us followed them. After passing by several identical wooden doors, we finally stopped at the end of the hallway in front of the last wooden door in the whole place.

"This is where the footsteps came from, guys," Dan said.

"You sure about that? How can you be absolutely sure that the footsteps came from behind that door?" Pitt asked.

"It's a good guess. It sounded pretty far away when we heard it in the kitchen," Decks explained.

"I don't know, guys... what if Granny is behind that door? What if she's going to take us all down as soon as we open it?! I'm scared. I don't want to go in!" Tina said, clearly panicking at the thought of what was to come.

None of us wanted to admit it, but we all agreed with Tina. Nobody wanted to face Granny. There was a long, silent moment in which no one said a word. You could almost have cut the tension in the air with a knife! It was Decks who eventually broke the silence.

"Look, guys, there's no other choice. We've got to go in there. We can't just stay here forever."

Everyone knew that Decks was right, but nobody wanted to admit it. Everyone felt safer in the hallway, but we couldn't stay here forever, right? It was a crazy idea. We had to go in, whether we liked it or not.

Everyone silently nodded their heads and gave Decks the go signal to kick the door down. We readied the kitchen utensils that we had grabbed from the kitchen earlier and prepared for the worst. Decks took a deep breath one last time and kicked the door down with so much force that it flew across the entire room.

"Freeze!" Decks shouted.

Freeze? I'm thinking this dude must have been a cop before he got into this mess with the rest of us! Maybe he a cop from another server or something. Someone who was so calm and commanding in a crisis had to have had some kind of training. I suddenly felt embarrassed. I was a new cop at Mad City, and I hadn't done anything great so far; I'd just ended up in this mess.

We followed Decks into the room and looked around anxiously. There was nothing here. It was completely empty, and there was no proof that Granny or Carlos had ever even been here. The only thing inside the small room was a really strange-looking, dirty, patterned carpet hung on one of the walls.

"There's no one here," Pitt remarked.

"Thank you, Captain Obvious," Shelby said with a sarcastic tone in his voice.

Pitt glared at Shelby but didn't reply. Everyone was busy investigating the small room and looking for clues, hoping to find any sort of sign that could lead them to Carlos, and hopefully the exit.

"There's nothing here. How could the footsteps have come from this room? They must have come from one of those other rooms we just passed," Casey said.

"Keep looking, guys. There's got to be something in here... like maybe a hidden drawer or door somewhere," Decks insisted.

I stared at the strange, dusty old carpet that hung on the wall and placed my finger on my chin. It was literally the only thing in the room, and I wondered if it were some kind of clue or something. I touched the carpet with my hand; it felt really old and ragged, obviously, but I could also feel something else. Something strange.

"Guys... I think... I think there's something beyond this carpet," I shouted.

The others quickly turned their attention to the carpet in question. Decks closely inspected the carpet like it were some kind of criminal and grabbed one of its ends.

"Only one way to find out," he said.

Decks quickly pulled the carpet with all of his strength, revealing the wall underneath... and a hidden door. It was a really narrow door, so small in fact that I couldn't imagine someone as big as Decks being able to fit through it.

"A hidden door!" Pitt exclaimed triumphantly.

"Again, thank you, Captain Obvious," Shelby replied.

"What's your problem, man? Why are you always cutting me out like that?" Pitt said angrily. I could tell that the tension between these two was increasing at an alarming rate.

"Ohh... I don't know. Maybe it's because you keep telling us things we already know?"

"Well, Mister Genius Pants, how come I

haven't heard you share with us a magic solution that'll get us out of this place?!" Pitt fired back.

"I've got one for you--"

"That's enough!" Decks shouted.

Decks's voice echoed throughout the entire room, quickly stopping Pitt and Shelby in their tracks. Decks was a big dude, and one you probably didn't want to make angry.

"Fighting each other is not going to get us out of this house! We need to work together to get out of this mess! Now if you two want to throw down and get into a fist fight, then be my guests! But you're both going to be left here if you do, so good luck dealing with that nutcase Granny on your own!" Decks cried.

"He started it!" Pitt responded childishly.

Decks gave Pitt a glare that could have sent a

lion shaking in its boots. Pitt got the message and pretty much zipped his mouth from that point on.

The silence was soon broken once again though as all of us suddenly heard the faint sound of a person crying for help. It was coming from beyond the small door, and we all knew that we had to get in there whether we wanted to or not.

"That sounded like Carlos!" Casey said.

Decks let out a deep sigh and prepared his leg for another kick. He thrust his foot forward and the small white door immediately caved in. It tumbled down the staircase for what seemed like forever until we finally heard it land deep down in the basement.

I've got a lot of horrible memories of that crazy staircase. It was narrow and small, just like the door, and the damp and cold gave it a weird smell. The old and awful-smelling walls were made of stone and it felt like they were about to eat you up and collapse in on each other at the same time.

Everyone in the room gulped and nodded their heads. We all knew that there was a difficult task ahead of us.

"I guess we've got to go down there now," Tina said nervously.

## Entry #4

# Into the Depths of the Stone Dungeon.

Decks nodded and headed through the door first, although that probably wasn't such a good idea. As the largest one of our group, I noticed that he had a hard time squeezing through the door to the narrow staircase, and an even harder time going down the stairs. Everyone took Decks's lead and began to descend down the stairs into the cold depths of Granny's creepy house. The air seemed to get thicker and colder with every step that we took.

After climbing down the stairs for what seemed like an eternity, we finally reached the bottom and saw a large hallway that looked remarkably similar to the one above, although the walls were made of stone. There were some torches placed on the walls and there were a number of identical wooden doors all placed next to one another. It was another maze, and it was all part of Granny's creepy and evil plan.

"Well, this honestly doesn't look very different from the house upstairs," Shelby said.

"Yeah, you want to stay up there? Be my guest, dumb dumb!" Pitt sneered.

"Why you--"

Before Pitt could say anything further, Shelby lunged himself through the air and a fist fight broke out between the two of them. Pitt and Shelby were both throwing their fists wildly at each other, although I noticed that neither of them was landing any good shots. Clearly, neither of the men were fighters but were just really angry with one another. They had almost zero fighting skill and everyone in the room could tell.

Before things got any more out of hand, Decks plunged into the fight and quickly broke the two apart. Decks grabbed them both by their shirt collars and carried them like a sack of potatoes. Decks was very different to Pitt and Shelby; I could definitely tell that this dude knew what he was doing. Not only was he big, but he also knew how to use his size to his advantage. He probably fought in some martial arts training camp or something before he got into this mess. If there was anyone in the group that could stand a chance against Granny, it was him.

"All right, that's enough! Back it up, you

two! I've had just about enough of this nonsense!" Decks said loudly. His voice echoed throughout the entire stone hallway in a really creepy way.

"He keeps messing with me, dude!" Shelby fired back.

"He's the one who started it! He said I was dumb and that I kept mentioning the obvious!" Pitt retorted.

"Look, I don't care what your reasons are for fighting--"

"Uhh, guys..?"

All of us turned our attention to Danny SN who was literally trembling in his shoes. His outstretched finger pointed towards something dark in the hallway, and we immediately realized why Dan was so scared. Standing right there in the distance was Granny. She didn't say anything, but just stood there like some sort of creepy statue with her glowing red eyes. Pretty much everyone in the hallway was frozen with fear - even Decks. No one expected to see Granny like this, but then again, who were we kidding? Granny was going show up sooner or later, and it's not like she was going to tell us before she made her move.

"I-i-it's... G-Granny!" Tina said. She could barely finish her sentence and she sounded like she was about to break down with fear.

Decks quickly snapped out of his trance and dropped both Pitt and Shelby onto the cold, hard, stone ground. He set off running after Granny like a cheetah who had just spotted its next meal.

"Come here, you!" Decks shouted as he ran towards his target.

Just as Decks reached Granny and was about to give her a giant knuckle sandwich with his fist, Granny disappeared into thin air like some kind of weird and mystical ninja. Decks looked around confused - there was no trace of Granny anywhere now.

"H-how did she..? But I thought..."

"It's obviously a trick, Decks. She wants to confuse us into thinking that she's everywhere. She's probably using some kind of magic spell on us. We've got to keep going," Dan explained.

"But how? These doors all look the same, just like upstairs. And there might be traps beyond these doors," Decks replied.

"I have an idea," Dickie said.

Dickie had remained pretty quiet the entire time that we'd been here, so we were all surprised to finally hear him talk.

"Shoot."

"I counted all of the doors while you guys were fighting and all that... and I think I have a plan. There's eight of us here right now, yes? Tina, Decks, Noob, Dan, Casey, Shelby, Pitt and me. That's eight people and there are eight doors," Dickie explained.

"Ohh, I see where you're going with this... so if all of us open one door each, we can cover more distance and hopefully find some kind of exit out of this place. Smart!" Shelby told Dickie.

Dickie smiled and nodded. I had to admit, it was a pretty good plan alright. While the rest of us had been busy panicking, Dickie had actually hatched a well-thought-out plan.

"N-no way! I'm not opening any of those doors! What if Granny's waiting on the other side of the door that I open?!" Tina said nervously.

"You have to, Tina. It's the only way we can

cover more ground and get out of here," Pitt replied calmly.

"He's right. And besides, if she does show up when you open your door, just call for help. I'll come crashing in and I'll beat her up for all that she's done to us!" Decks said angrily.

Decks's last remark seemed to give Tina a little bit of confidence. She took a deep breath and picked out one out of the eight wooden doors in the hallway. The rest of us picked our own, and soon we were all standing in front of our respective doors, waiting to open them at the same time.

"Everyone ready?" Decks called.

"Yeah."

"Ready."

"I'm good."

"Let's do this!"

"O-okay."

"Let's go."

"Yes."

We pushed open our individual doors slowly. The doors all creaked at the same time, and the creaking sounds echoed throughout the entire hallway. Nobody said a word for a few minutes until Dan finally broke the silence.

"My room is... empty. And it's got another door ahead."

"Mine too," Pitt said.

"Same here."

"My room's empty too!" Tina added.

Unfortunately, my room wasn't empty, and it didn't seem to lead to nowhere like the others. Inside the room was a long and narrow hall. The hall was dimly-lit and I could barely see anything, but it seemed to lead to somewhere.

I guess this is the part where you can squarely blame me for my own misfortune. Rather than calling out to Decks and the others for assistance, I decided to explore the place for myself. Call it a cop's intuition or maybe his pride; whatever it was, I figured I could handle whatever I bumped into. Of course, I was very wrong.

I hadn't walked far when I felt something large and metallic clamp down on my leg. It all happened so fast that it wasn't even painful. At least, not at first.

"What the...?"

I looked down and saw the large bear trap. It had sunk its metal teeth into my legs, and there was no way it was letting go. My leg was getting numb now and it was starting to really hurt. And that was when I saw the bear in front of me.

Yeah, everything had led to this terrible moment. I figured that I was going to die right here. I was going to die, not outside in the crazy streets of Mad City, chasing robbers or anything like that. No, I was going to die being eaten alive by a bear, a victim of one of Granny's most infamous traps.

Well, fate, and Decks, had other ideas.

The bear was running towards me at full speed, but Decks moved even faster. Yep, Decks. He came out of nowhere and slammed into the bear, the two of them colliding like two trains running right into each other. I guess I was wrong earlier. Someone actually did hear me call out for help, and that person was Decks.

Decks and the bear were locked together in a rolling death grip. Neither of them were about to let go. I felt helpless as I watched the two of them fighting for my life, but what could I do? The bear trap was locked firmly on my leg.

After what seemed like an eternity, the two of them stopped struggling. The bear went limp, and Decks stood up. He was all bloody, but he was still alive.

"Decks! You did it!"

"Yeah, and I don't want to do anything like that again."

"No argument here, but how did you defeat that bear?"

Decks held out a piece of broken glass. It was razor sharp and covered in the bear's blood.

"I managed to pick up a glass shard in this place. Figured it would come in handy sooner or later. Apparently, I was right."

"No argument here again. But I guess I'm done for, anyway."

"What do you mean?"

I pointed at my bloody leg and the bear trap.

"I'm trapped in this bear trap. Unless you've got a sledgehammer or something like it, I'm not going anywhere. You might as well use that shard of glass on me now. End me now so I won't be a liability to you and the others."

Decks shook his head.

"There ain't no way I'm leaving anyone here behind. I may not have a sledgehammer, but I might have something just as good."

"What do you mean?"

Decks whipped out a rusty key from his person.

"Where did you get that?" I asked.

"Remember when I saw Granny earlier and I tried to punch her and I missed and she disappeared? Well, Dan said that it was all a trick, but it wasn't. Not in the way we thought. She was no illusion. That was the real Granny. I managed to get close enough to her to pick her dress."

I couldn't believe what I was hearing! To do something like that, Decks must have history as a minor thief or something like that.

"Pick her dress? You used to be a pickpocket or something?"

Decks smiled at me.

"Guilty as charged. You learn a lot of things growing up in the mean streets of Mad City."

I smiled at Decks.

"You sure you should be telling all of this to a cop?"

Decks smiled back at me, and shook his head.

"No, but I'm not going to let anyone die in a

place like this. I was a petty thief back in the day, not a killer. Now, let's just hope this key is the right fit for that bear trap. It could be the key to anything."

Decks bent down and used the small, rusty key on the trap. I heard it squeak as it turned. Decks fiddled with the key a little longer and soon I was free! I howled in pain.

Attracted to my cry of pain, everyone came rushing through the door.

"Whoa! That looks real bad!" Dan said.

"Move over. I used to be a doctor before all of this craziness."

It was Tina. She moved towards me and examined my wound.

"It's not that bad. Decks take off your shirt. I'll need you to tear it up. I can tie up the wound with it and minimize the bleeding."

Decks took off his shirt and ripped it up, just as Tina had said.. Tina wrapped the cloth around my bleeding leg, fashioning a crude bandage to stop the bleeding.

"There, that should stop the bleeding. You're lucky, Noob. Although that bear trap looked menacing, it wasn't meant to kill. The real killer would have been that bear lying in front of you. A little real medication in some hospital, and you'll be fine- assuming you get out of here alive, of course."

"Of course. And Tina, Decks, thanks. I owe you both."

Decks shook his head.

"Forget it. Now, let's get moving. I want to get out of here."

We went back to the business of exploring the other rooms that had been opened. Pretty soon, everyone realized that the room behind their door simply led to another room... and another... and another... and another. It was like a never-ending maze of doors and rooms that simply didn't end. A true labyrinth. This Granny person was crazy indeed!

"How are we going to get out now? This is endless!" Pitt cried.

Before anyone could reply, the sound of Decks's loud voice crackling inside the weird maze filled the air.

Entry #5

# Two Down, Seven More to Go...

"Guys! Guys! Come here! Carlos! He's here!"

Everyone quickly retraced their steps and made their way to Decks's location. It wasn't easy- the maze was really confusing and every room looked the same- but the sound of Decks's voice eventually led us to our destination.

"Carlos! Carlos! Wake up, man!" Decks shouted.

Stepping inside the room, we quickly noticed one thing that made this room stand out from the rest: there was a boiling pit of lava that separated us from Carlos! The pit was the entire width of the room, and the only way to get across was to jump over it. I suddenly felt a wave of nervousness overcome me; I wasn't good at jumping! One mistake and I'd fall to my death in the lava pit! Oh man, this was bad news!

We all kept calling Carlos' name but he didn't respond. It looked as if he had a big red lump on his head; clearly Granny had whacked him pretty hard with something.

Carlos eventually regained consciousness and awoke slowly, looking really confused and dazed. I doubt he even had any idea where he was.

"H-huh... w-where am I..? Arghh! My head hurts!" Carlos said as he sat up and began rubbing his temples.

"Carlos! Thank goodness you're awake! Can

you hear me?" Decks shouted.

"Yeah, man... I can hear you loud and clear. What's going on?"

"You're in Granny's house, remember? I'm Decks, and you were trapped with everyone else in the group! Then the lights went out and Granny kidnapped you!" Decks reminded him.

"Y-yeah... I think I can remember now... I don't remember how I get here in this room though. And what's that boiling pit of lava doing there?" Carlos said.

"I don't know. We're at the very bottom of Granny's house right now, probably the basement level. Do you think you can jump across here? We'll try to find an exit together," Decks said.

"Oh yeah, for sure. Pffft. Look at that lava pit. This will be easy. You guys do know that

I'm a decorated basketball player, right?" Carlos said arrogantly. Clearly, the knock to his head hadn't got rid of that attitude problem of his.

We all looked at each other and shook our heads.

"Aww, come on! Don't tell me you guys don't play Basketblox! I'm the biggest star there! I'm totally the best basketball player ever! Everyone is always talking about my slick basketball skills. Ever see the time when I scored a huge slam dunk--?"

"Would you just shut up and jump already?!" Dan cried.

Carlos shrugged his shoulders and stood up. He squatted down low, readying himself for the big jump across the lava pit. All of us were pretty sure that he'd make it across after his boasts about being a good basketball player.

But Carlos made one very big mistake.

He forgot to tie his shoelaces!

Rather than jumping across the pool, Carlos instead slipped forward into the boiling lava. Everyone in the group shouted and stared in horror as Carlos started to burn right in front of our eyes.

"Carlos! Nooooo!" Decks shouted desperately.

Decks reached out his hand in order to pull Carlos from the pit, but it was too late. In just seconds, Carlos' body had totally disappeared.

"Oh my gosh! Nooo! This is getting crazy! I've got to get out of here!" Tina screamed as sweat trickled down her forehead.

Tina turned back towards the door and started to make a run for it. She hadn't noticed though the small pebble in front of her. In her panic, she slipped on the stone and quickly slid backward into the boiling lava pit, just like Carlos before her.

"Arghhh! Help me!" Tina screamed desperately.

Tina slid into the lava pit so quickly that Decks didn't have time to save her. First Carlos and now Tina?! This was getting out of hand. Granny was probably laughing somewhere in the dark about this. This was not good. Not good at all.

"Noooo! Darn it!" Decks cried.

"That's two down... seven more to go," Dickie said grimly.

"Why are you being so negative about this, man?! We'll get out of this alive, you'll see!" Shelby said.

I could tell that Shelby was also really scared but was doing his best not to show it. I had to admit though, Dickie was right. We were two people down and Granny probably didn't intend on letting any of us out of her madhouse. The big question was: who was going to be next? I gulped at the thought of being burned by Granny. I had to stay alive somehow... I had to get out of this place in one piece!

"Look, guys, everyone calm down! Look what happened to Tina when she started to panic! There's a way out of this place, but we just have to stay calm!" Decks shouted.

"Calm?! Are you serious, man? We just saw two people get burned alive because of Granny's traps! Who's to say we're not next?!" Pitt shouted desperately.

"You want to go jump in the lava pit? Then be my guest! But our best chance of surviving is by staying calm!" Decks fired back.

"Decks is right. Let's exit this room calmly

and slowly. There must be another room that leads to some sort of exit somewhere..." Dan insisted.

But there wasn't.

Once out of the boiling lava pit room, we thoroughly searched the other rooms in the hopes that we would find a door that would lead us out of Granny's house. But there was no such door. All the rooms simply led on to other rooms, and finally, after what felt like hours of searching and opening doors, everyone gave up and realized that there was only one way out of the dungeon: through the lava pit.

"We've been searching these rooms for hours! They just lead to more rooms and even more rooms! This is crazy! We're going to starve to death down here if we don't do something soon!" Pitt said.

"For once, I've got to agree with you, Pitt.

We can't keep doing this forever. These rooms are just leading us nowhere. The only logical place to go now is across the lava pit. It's the only place we haven't explored yet," Shelby agreed.

Decks, strangely enough, was the only person who didn't seem to like the idea. I was surprised; he was the one in the group who seemed the bravest, despite all of the challenges we had faced so far.

"No, no, no! We're not going back there! There has to be a way out of this place in one of these rooms! Probably some kind of secret entrance just like that time where the carpet was hiding the door," Decks insisted.

"Look, Decks, we can't do this forever. We've been at this for hours now. There's clearly no trap door or secret entrance anywhere in these rooms; just concrete and even more concrete! We have to jump over the lava pit!

78

It's the only way!"

Decks sneered and shook his head.

"I think Shelby's right, Decks. We've already lost Carlos and Tina. We'll all lose each other here if we don't make our move!" I told him.

Decks reluctantly nodded his head. He obviously didn't like the idea, but what could he do? He was outnumbered six to one. None of us wanted to jump over the lava pit, but there was no other choice – it was either that or wait and starve to death. I'd sooner take my chances with the lava pit.

Danny SN was the first one to make the jump. His legs propelled him forward and up towards the other side. To be honest, I didn't think Dan would be able to make it, but he sure proved me wrong. I didn't think that someone who did mostly Youtube in his spare time would have the athletic skill to jump across a boiling pit of lava, but who was I to say? He did it, and he did it pretty well!

Decks went next. Jumping to the other side was nothing for Decks. His huge, muscular legs easily propelled him into the air and he landed with a loud thud on the concrete on the other side of the boiling lava pit. Decks had legs like the Incredible Hulk; it was no surprise that he was able to make the jump.

One by one, with a little bit of help from Decks and Dan, the others in the group also successfully made the jump. I was the last to attempt it and I was really scared. I mean, who wouldn't be? One wrong move and I would easily end up like Carlos or Tina.

"Come on, Noob, you can do it!" Casey called out.

"Yeah, don't worry about it. Everyone else made it. We've got your back," Decks shouted.

I looked down at the boiling pit of lava one last time and took a deep breath.

"Here goes nothing," I thought to myself.

I squatted down and pushed off from the ground as hard as I could. It was a pretty good attempt, and I would have easily made it past the pit. There was one problem though...

I slipped!

I was just as clumsy as Tina and Carlos. I quickly found myself falling fast towards the pit of lava. I knew that it was the end so I simply closed my eyes and prepared for the worst.

Entry #6

# Don't Slip, Don't Fall!

Just when I thought that I was about to get burned alive, I felt someone's hands grip my shoulders. It was Decks. His grip on me was really, really tight as he attempted to save me from my fiery fate. Think of a giant, eight-foot crab that just grabbed you with its giant iron claws or something.

"Oh no you don't! I've already lost two people; I'm not about to lose another one!" Decks cried.

With his great strength, Decks lifted me up

from the pit of lava as if I was as light as a feather and tossed me into the concrete wall. I felt the hard stone wall slam against my shoulder, but hey, it was a lot better than getting burned alive.

"Ouch!"

"Sorry about that, Noob. I had to make sure you were as far away from the lava pit as possible."

"Great! We've all made it. We'd better keep going... we just might make it out of this alive!" Dan said happily.

Little did we know that the lava pit was just the first of many traps that Granny had in store for us...

We looked around for an exit and noticed a small door behind us. It creaked as the others had earlier as we opened it cautiously. But what we saw beyond the door definitely surprised us. This one wasn't like the others where the rooms simply led to other rooms... no, this one was very different.

It was a really, really, really big room... or should I say, pit. Where the floor should have been, there was only a gigantic hole, so deep that it appeared endless. The only way we could get across was to walk over a narrow wooden beam. There were no rails to hold on to; we simply had to balance ourselves and hope that we wouldn't fall into the deep pit below.

We all gulped and hesitated at the sight of the small walkway. It was so narrow that you had to place one foot on the beam at a time or else you'd fall below.

"What is this?!" Shelby cried out.

"It looks like some kind of really, really narrow bridge... I think I can see a door at the end of it though," Pitt shouted.

84

"This is insane! That walkway is way too narrow! We'll never get across!" Casey panicked.

"Not if we do it really, really, really slowly," Decks said reassuringly.

Decks was probably going to have the hardest time getting across the bridge since he was the biggest. He would have to balance his weight on the walkway and that wouldn't be easy.

After a few minutes of silence, Decks broke the tension in the air.

"Look, we've got this far, right? I mean, we found the secret dungeon in the house, we found Carlos, we made it across the lava pit and now we're here. There's no turning back. We have to move," Decks said grimly.

"This is all part of Granny's evil plan... we've got to make her pay somehow, guys!" I said.

"Don't worry, dude. I'm sure we'll get out of this place, one way or another," Dan told me reassuringly.

Dan smiled at me and that was all the encouragement I needed to get across. I mean, hey, if a big Youtube star believed in me and in the rest of us, then why shouldn't we believe in ourselves?

Decks took his first steps on the narrow walkway and the rest of us quickly followed him. Each of us cautiously took one step at a time, making our way across the walkway very slowly. One wrong step and we could all fall to our doom.

Our strategy seemed to be working; I was surprised to see that we were all making pretty good progress despite the narrowness of the walkway. In fact, I could clearly see the door on the other side which meant that we were already halfway across. Everything was going great...

Until Decks slipped.

His foot was just too big. It caught the edge of the narrow walkway and the rest happened so fast that I can't remember much of it to be honest with you guys.

As Decks fell, I saw Pitt, Shelby and even Casey grab a hold of him to try and pull him back up onto the walkway... but Decks was just too heavy. Dickie, Dan and I watched in horror as four of our new friends fell to their doom in the deep, black pit. We heard their cries as they fell deeper and deeper into the endless cavern of darkness.

"Noooooo!"

"Heeeeeeelp!"

"Ahhhhh!"

I tried to reach out for their hands but it was

too late. Dan instinctively pulled me back and gripped my shoulders.

"No! Don't even try, dude! You'll just fall down as well! It's too late for them! We've got to keep going! We're almost across, man!" Dan said.

"But those guys were our friends!" I protested.

"So were Carlos and Tina. It's just the three of us now. And the only way to help them now is by making that evil, crazy old coot pay," Dickie said angrily.

He was right. There was no way we could save our friends now. It was much too late for them. Granny had to pay for all of this, one way or another.

After a few more tense moments, Dickie, Dan and I successfully crossed the narrow walkway and made it over to the wooden door. All three of us breathed a sigh of relief, and boy was I thankful that I was one of the lucky ones who had made it this far.

## Entry #7

# The Final Fight.

"This is it, guys. This is the moment when we put an end to all of this", I said to Dickie and Dan.

"Wait, what? How can you be sure that this is the last room? We walked through countless rooms earlier; how can you be so sure that this is the one?" Dan asked.

"Well, uhh... I don't know, really. I've just got this gut feeling that this is it. Yeah, maybe I'm wrong, but whatever. Just get ready, guys," I told them both.

Dickie and Danny took out the kitchen materials they had chosen earlier and readied themselves for a fight. Dickie took out the frying pan and Dan took out a large, wooden spoon. I hadn't noticed Dan taking the spoon earlier; he must've snuck it out just as we were about to leave.

I took out my own weapon of choice... the rolling pin. A frying pan, a wooden spoon and a rolling pin... not exactly destructive weapons of war, but better than trying to fight with just our bare hands, I guess.

All three of us took a few deep breaths before opening the door and stepping inside.

Through the door was a stone room, just like all the others, although this time it was much bigger. Much, much, much bigger. There were no narrow walkways, boiling lava pits or extra doors inside. Nope, it was just a really large stone room with four torches attached to the walls on each side of us. And who was in the middle of it? Yes, you guessed it. The villain of the night: Granny herself.

"Well now, boys… I'm surprised you made it this far. I didn't think that anyone would actually get past all my traps and make it here…," she said menacingly. There was something weird about the way in which she spoke; her high-pitched voice made her sound a lot like a bird talking.

"You're going to pay for all the people you've taken down, Granny!" Danny SN shouted.

"We'll see about that. See, now that you're here, you can freely exit the house through a final door that's hidden within this room… but it will only show itself if you can beat me!" Granny said, letting out an evil laugh.

Danny SN and Dickie had heard enough. They'd suffered enough and they'd had enough. They weren't about to talk to this crazy old coot any longer. Both of them charged towards her with their kitchen utensils in their hands, ready to fight.

But Granny was a lot faster than anyone had expected. She moved like a ghost and immediately knocked out Dan and Dickie with her infamous baseball bat with just one blow to the head. I hadn't done anything yet and I was literally shaking in my boots. I was next, and I knew the end was near.

"W-wait, p-please! Have mercy! I used to have a totally awesome life in Robloxia! I should never have become a cop! Never! I just can't do this kind of stuff! I'm too young to get whacked in the head with a baseball bat by some creepy old woman!" I pleaded.

Yeah, I know how that came out. I looked and sounded like a total wuss. A coward. A yellowbelly. The list of awful names could go on and on. But I was terrified and I just couldn't help myself. Being in that situation was just too horrifying; no amount of training could have prepared me to face the monster that was Granny.

But Granny didn't care. She didn't care if I, or any of her victims, were scared stiff. In fact, she enjoyed all of this. Granny was some sick and twisted creature that enjoyed the suffering and fear of others. If she was once human, she certainly was not anymore; she was something else entirely now. And I would have to face this monster with nothing but my rolling pin.

She dived straight at me like an eagle that had spotted its target. Without thinking, I quickly pulled out the rolling pin that I had taken earlier and used it as a shield against Granny's attacks. I know what you're thinking: what good could a rolling pin do against a baseball bat? I know, it was a silly idea... but it actually worked. Granny was about to nail me but she stopped dead in her tracks when she caught a glimpse of the rolling pin.

"Nooo! What are you doing with my rolling pin?! That's the same rolling pin I used to use to make cookies for Slendrina! Give it back!" Granny ordered.

Granny grabbed the end of the rolling pin and began to pull. I pulled back, and a small tug of war ensued between the two of us. While we were both fighting for the rolling pin, Dan and Dickie regained consciousness. With Granny so distracted, they knew that this was their best chance.

I watched them both stand and lunge themselves straight at Granny. Granny never saw it coming. Dickie began whacking her with the frying pan and Dan began pummeling her ribs with his wooden spoon. It was a really strange sight seeing two guys beating up a crazy old lady with kitchen utensils, but I can't say she didn't deserve it... not after what she had done to our friends earlier.

There was no escape for Granny now and she knew it. After being pummeled for over five minutes, Granny fell to the floor and collapsed. She had taken a pounding from Dan and Dickie, and she was done.

"W-what happened?! Is it over?" Dan said as he looked around, still partially concussed and confused about what had happened.

"I think we beat her," Dickie said.

"Yeah, guys! You totally did it! You beat that crazy old coot!" I said.

You could hear the joy and excitement in my voice. I was so relieved and thankful that this was all over. I had just about had it with this terrible place and the many death traps inside. The dark corners, the rotting floors, the traps, the overgrown spiders, the large holes... all that was done. We were all going to survive our encounter with Granny!

Or were we?

It was a little too early for us to celebrate, but we all realized this too late. It turned out Granny wasn't done with us. Not by a long shot.

Dickie didn't even see it coming. None of us did. That old windbag moved so fast, it seemed unnatural for, well, an old windbag. Out of nowhere, she whacked Dickie from behind with that large bat of hers, a lot harder and with more force than before. I knew that Dickie was not getting up from this hit. Another one of us down, and in the most unexpected manner.

"Dickie, no!"

Dickie wasn't answering, and he wasn't

moving on the ground. Granny had taken another victim.

I raised my rolling pin to try and smash her the way she had smashed Dickie, but it was no use. Granny moved fast and swung hard. Her baseball bat struck my rolling pin and she snapped it in two. Dan and I couldn't believe it. How could an old woman do something like that? Granny had unbelievable strength. Then again, she had a lot of unbelievable stuff going for her. Like I said before, she was like some kind of inhuman creature that was anything but normal.

I rushed towards her but Granny was too fast. She struck me in the gut with her baseball bat and I instantly felt the wind knocked out of me. I couldn't breathe, and I doubled up in pain, collapsing on the ground and clutching my stomach.

"You crazy old monster! You're going to pay

for all of this! You're going to pay!"

It was Dan. He was enraged and frustrated now. He couldn't believe that Granny was still somehow standing; he had to do something. Dan rushed at Granny, which really was not the smartest thing to do. In fact, it was just about the worst thing Dan could have done.

Dan ran right smack onto Granny's baseball bat. She whacked him so hard that Dan went flying. Once Dan was knocked down, Granny began hitting him over and over again with her bat. She didn't stop. Not even after Dan stopped moving.

"Dan! Stop! No!"

I was still lying on the floor, in too much pain to even try and stop Granny. The pain in my stomach was too intense to even try to move.

After what seemed like an eternity, Granny

turned towards me.

"Both your friends are done for, fool. Now, it is your turn."

Granny walked towards me. I was in too much pain to get up from the floor and she knew it. She wasn't even rushing towards me. I realized that she was going to take her time with me. She was going to take my life slowly and enjoy every minute of my suffering. What kind of a monster was I dealing with here?

"You're all going to pay. All of you," Granny said.

Her voice sounded like something between broken glass and a crow cawing. It was hoarse and could barely be heard.

"Why are you doing this? What did we ever do to you?"

Granny shook her head. She was in no mood

to give me answers. She was just in the mood to kill me.

Once again, I pretty much thought that I was done for. But that was when the unexpected happened.

"Hey, ugly! I'm not through with you yet!"

I heard the familiar voice from behind Granny. It couldn't be? How was this possible? Granny turned around, her face a picture of shock. Behind her stood Decks.

"You? You fell into the bottomless pit! How are you even still alive?"

Granny couldn't believe it, and neither could I. I had seen Decks fall into that bottomless pit with our other friends with my own eyes. Granny was right: Decks should have been done for, but he wasn't. Somehow, he had managed to climb out, and he now stood in front of Granny, face-to-face.

I could see that there was something different about Decks. He looked a lot more haggard and beaten up than last time I'd seen him, as if he had gone through a meat grinder and survived. But there was also something more. There was something different about the way Decks stared at Granny. All of us throughout our terrible ordeal had felt fear, and for good reason. We had all been transported into that crazy house where no one returned. We had watched our friends disappear. We had come face to face with Granny. It was natural to be afraid.

But Decks was no longer afraid. There was no fear in his eyes. He stared down Granny, as if his eyes could burn holes through her. Decks wasn't backing down; he was now fearless. Falling through that bottomless pit and managing to climb out had changed Decks.

"No one's ever survived falling down the bottomless pit. No one!"

Decks grinned and laughed softly at Granny. It seemed as if he were laughing at death itself. Hearing Decks, I actually felt more afraid of him at that moment than of Granny.

"Yeah, well, I guess I'm no one then."

Decks whipped out a pack of cards from his body. He hadn't had them on his person before. At the sight of them, Granny seemed genuinely terrified.

"The cards of fate! How did you get ahold of them?"

Decks shook his head.

"I don't need to answer any of your questions."

Decks pulled out a card from the deck and tossed it at Granny. He tossed the card so fast, I barely managed to follow it with my eyes. The card struck Granny's hand. It cut her, and she drew back in pain. Granny dropped her baseball bat, and clutched her wounded hand.

"Yaaah! You cut me!"

"I'm going to do a lot more than just cut you, Granny. You're done for!"

Decks whipped out another card and tossed it Granny's way. The second card was more powerful than the first. It struck Granny right in the chest and something unbelievable happened. Granny exploded. It was as if Decks had tossed a bomb her way.

It was a small, controlled explosion that had just enough power to take Granny out. The entire house remained untouched, and I was also unharmed. When the smoke cleared, there was nothing left of Granny. It was just Decks standing in front of me.

"Whoa! Decks! You're... you're alive," I said.

Decks shrugged his shoulders. He still had the deck of fate held firmly in one hand.

"Yeah, I am."

"That's incredible! You're alive and you killed Granny! That's... I just can't believe it!"

I was at a loss for words. I couldn't believe what I had just seen. I had really thought that I would never see Decks again.

"Hey, maybe I'm just a lot tougher to kill than I look."

Decks was being coy, but I had to know how he managed to survive such a fall.

"How did you do it, Decks? How did you survive that fall? And what are those cards you picked up?"

I was eager to get some answers, but Decks was reluctant to provide them. He just shook his head and stared at me. There was no hate in his eyes, but his gaze was as firm as it was with Granny earlier. It was clear that Decks didn't want to give any answers, and I decided to just leave it at that. After all, it was hard to argue with a man who had cards like that. Decks had just taken out Granny with those things. He had the cards stacked in his favor, literally.

"All right, I guess I'll leave it at that."

"Granny's done. We should be able to get out of here now."

Decks spoke as if he knew the house very well now. He spoke as if he were referring to an old enemy whose habits he knew in detail. I guess the fall had changed him in many ways that I could barely imagine.

We both suddenly caught a glimpse of a door that seemed to have magically appeared out of nowhere. This door was different from the others. Through its transparent windows we could see the most awesome thing ever. I immediately recognized the buildings and structures outside; this was the skyline of Mad City. I don't know how it had happened, but somehow the house was just outside of Mad City now. I'll never fully understand that house, or Granny; it was as if both were magical things that existed out of pure evil. Now that Granny was done, the house had lost its grip on us, and Decks and I were both free to go home. We had achieved freedom at last, and it was waiting for us just beyond the wooden door. We did it! We beat Granny and put her in her place!

"It's over. It's really over then. We can finally walk out of here," I said.

"Yeah, I guess it is. We were the only ones to make it out alive."

Decks spoke with a heavy heart. He sounded

sad and almost guilty that he had survived. I really couldn't blame him.

We stepped outside and saw Mad City up ahead. It would be a bit of a walk to get there, but Decks and I didn't mind. We were just relieved to still be alive.

"Is she really gone for good? Granny I mean," I asked.

Decks shrugged his shoulders.

"Granny and that house were like evil spirits or something. They can appear anywhere, and you can't really kill something like that."

We turned around and saw that the house had vanished. It had just been standing there moments ago, and now it was gone. Decks's words were already making sense.

"What are you going to do now?" I asked Decks.

Decks smiled at me and nodded towards the pack of cards he still carried in his hand.

"I think I'll put these things to good use. After all, I did almost die back there to get them. A cop and a petty thief, the only survivors of Granny's house of horrors. Kind of ironic, isn't it?"

I couldn't argue with Decks. It was pretty strange that the two of us would be the only survivors. Strange, but it had to just be a coincidence, right? I mean, it wasn't like I would ever see Decks again.

"You're not going to go after me after all of this, are you?" Decks asked.

I smiled and shook my head.

"No way. You saved my life back there. Besides, I've probably got a lot more pressing things to do now."

Decks held up the deck of fate with pride.

Something told me that this would not be the last I would see of him.

"Pressing stuff? Like what?"

I pointed at my leg, the blood showing through the makeshift bandage. It hadn't really bothered me too much up until now; I guess I had been too scared the entire time to focus on it.

"Taking care of my leg, for one thing. And then I think I'll continue my work on the force. Hopefully, I won't ever have to see Granny again. Hopefully neither of us will."

And that's how the crazy adventure with Granny ended.

Sure, we may have lost a lot of friends in the process, but hey, they probably just respawned somewhere else and are living their best lives right now.

The important thing was that we did

something that so many other people had failed to do: we defeated Granny, escaped her house and lived to tell the tale.

If you enjoyed this book, please leave a review on Amazon! It would really help me with the series.

Best,

Robloxia Kid

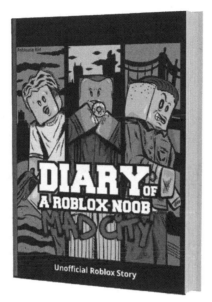

## *to be continued in...*

**DIARY OF A ROBLOX NOOB: MAD CITY**

https://geni.us/madcity

Made in the USA
San Bernardino, CA
29 January 2020

63741242R00076